# LET'S SPEAK FRENCH!
## A FIRST BOOK OF WORDS

VIKING
Published by the Penguin Group
Penguin Books USA Inc., 375 Hudson Street, New York, New York 10014, U.S.A.
Penguin Books Ltd, 27 Wrights Lane, London W8 5TZ, England
Penguin Books Australia Ltd, Ringwood, Victoria, Australia
Penguin Books Canada Ltd, 10 Alcorn Avenue, Toronto, Ontario, Canada M4V 3B2
Penguin Books (N.Z.) Ltd, 182–190 Wairau Road, Auckland 10, New Zealand

Penguin Books Ltd, Registered Offices: Harmondsworth, Middlesex, England

First published in Canada as
*The Kids Can Press French & English Word Book*
by The Kids Can Press, 1991
First published in the United States by Viking,
a division of Penguin Books USA Inc., 1993

10  9  8  7  6  5  4  3  2  1

Library of Congress Cataloging-in-Publication Data
Let's speak French: a first book of words /
edited by Katherine Farris; illustrated by Linda Hendry.     p.     cm.
English and French.
Rev. ed. of: The Kids Can Press French & English word book.
Summary: Labeled pictues in French and English introduce vocabulary
for everyday scenes in the home, school, and neighborhood, and
essential concepts such as colors, numbers, and opposites.
I S B N  0 - 6 7 0 - 8 5 0 4 2 - X
1. French language—Vocabulary—Juvenile literature.  2. French language—
Textbooks for foreign speakers—English—Juvenile literature.
[1. French language—Vocabulary.]  I. Farris, Katherine.
II. Hendry, Linda, ill.  III. Kids Can Press French & English word book.
PC2445.L39  1993   448.2′421—dc20     92-41737  CIP  AC

Printed in Hong Kong     Set in Century Schoolbook

# LET'S SPEAK FRENCH!

## A FIRST BOOK OF WORDS

EDITED BY **KATHERINE FARRIS**

ILLUSTRATED BY **LINDA HENDRY**

**VIKING**

# Bienvenue chez moi
# Welcome to my house

des bardeaux
shingles

un toit
roof

une chambre
bedroom

une fenêtre
window

un mur
wall

un porche
porch

un salon
living room

un sous-sol
basement

un perron
front steps

une cheminée
chimney

un garage
garage

une salle de bain
bathroom

un escalier
stairs

une jardinière
flower box

une porte
door

une cuisine
kitchen

une corde à linge
clothes line

ne salle à manger
dining room

un jardin
garden

un portillon
gate

une clôture
fence

## Voici ma famille
## Here's my family

un grand-père
grandfather

un cousin
cousin

une cousine
cousin

un père
father

un frère
brother

une mère
mother

un bébé
baby

un chien
dog

une soeur
sister

une grand-mère
grandmother

une tante
aunt

un oncle
uncle

une nièce
niece

un neveu
nephew

des jumelles
twins

un chat
cat

une arrière-grand-mère
great grandmother

un arrière-grand-père
great grandfather

# C'est le matin
# It's morning

**se brosser les dents**
brush your teeth

**prendre un bain**
take a bath

**dormir**
sleep

**lire**
read

**s'asseoir**
sit

**faire frire un oeuf**
fry an egg

**manger**
eat

**boire**
drink

**tondre la pelouse**
mow the lawn

**arroser les plantes**
water the plants

**se battre**
fight

**monter l'escalier**
go up the stairs

prendre une douche
take a shower

se sécher les cheveux
dry your hair

repasser
iron

pleurer
cry

marcher
walk

tomber
fall

rire
laugh

regarder la télé
watch TV

descendre l'escalier
go down the stairs

9

Bonjour!
Good morning!

un blouson
jacket

un chapeau
hat

des bottes
boots

une chemise
shirt

des souliers
shoes

un peignoir
bathrobe

des chaussettes
socks

des lacets
shoelaces

une robe
dress

une culotte
underpants

des chaussures de sport
running shoes

un sweat-shirt
sweatshirt

un maillot de corps
undershirt

un tee-shirt
T-shirt

une jupe
skirt

un short
shorts

un pantalon
pants

une chemise de nuit
nightgown

un pull-over
sweater

un gilet
vest

un bonnet
hat

un pyjama
pajamas

une moufle
mitten

des pantoufles
slippers

une écharpe
scarf

un manteau
coat

une ceinture
belt

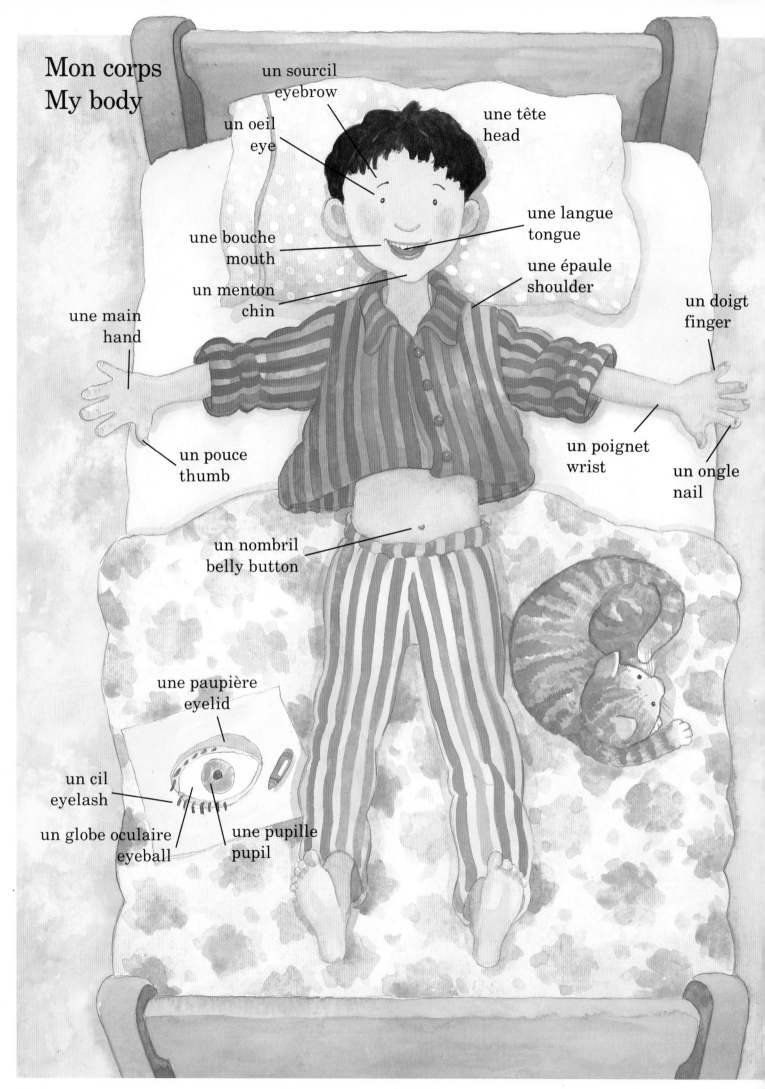

Mon corps
My body

un sourcil
eyebrow

un oeil
eye

une tête
head

une langue
tongue

une bouche
mouth

une épaule
shoulder

un menton
chin

une main
hand

un doigt
finger

un pouce
thumb

un poignet
wrist

un ongle
nail

un nombril
belly button

une paupière
eyelid

un cil
eyelash

un globe oculaire
eyeball

une pupille
pupil

12

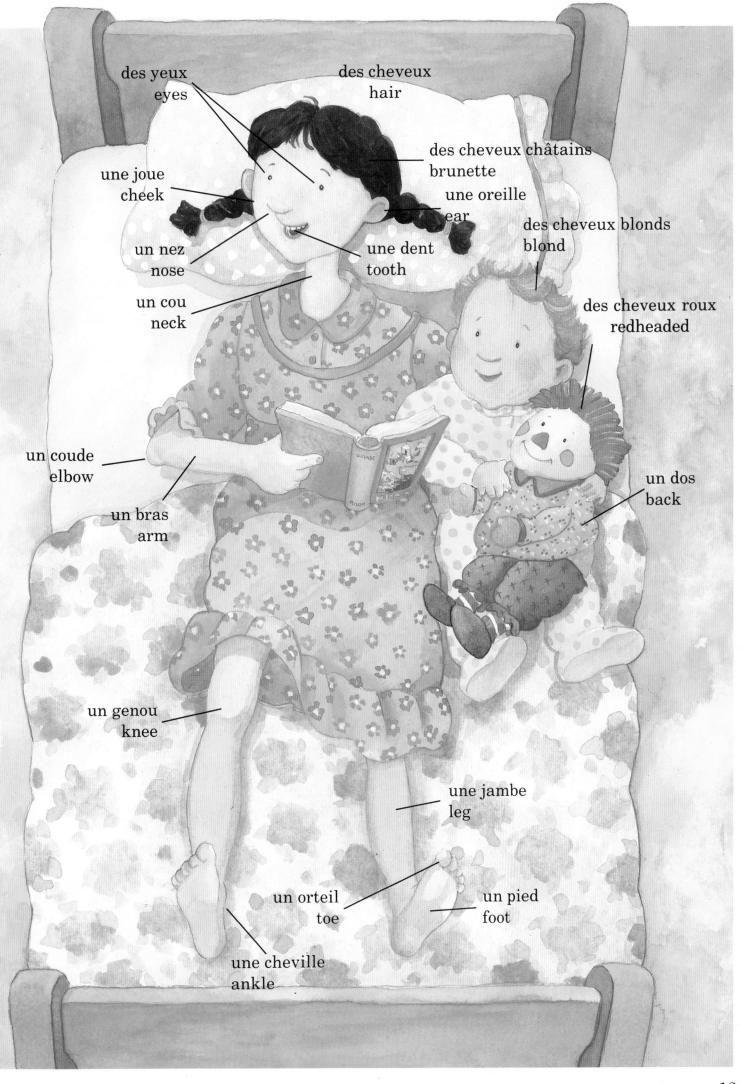

des yeux
eyes

des cheveux
hair

des cheveux châtains
brunette

une joue
cheek

une oreille
ear

des cheveux blonds
blond

un nez
nose

une dent
tooth

des cheveux roux
redheaded

un cou
neck

un coude
elbow

un dos
back

un bras
arm

un genou
knee

une jambe
leg

un orteil
toe

un pied
foot

une cheville
ankle

# On déjeune
# Breakfast time

un couteau
knife

une assiette
plate

une fourchette
fork

une cuillère
spoon

du beurre
butter

des croissants
croissants

une tasse
cup

un oeuf
egg

du sucre
sugar

du pain grillé
toast

une théière
teapot

un grille-pain
toaster

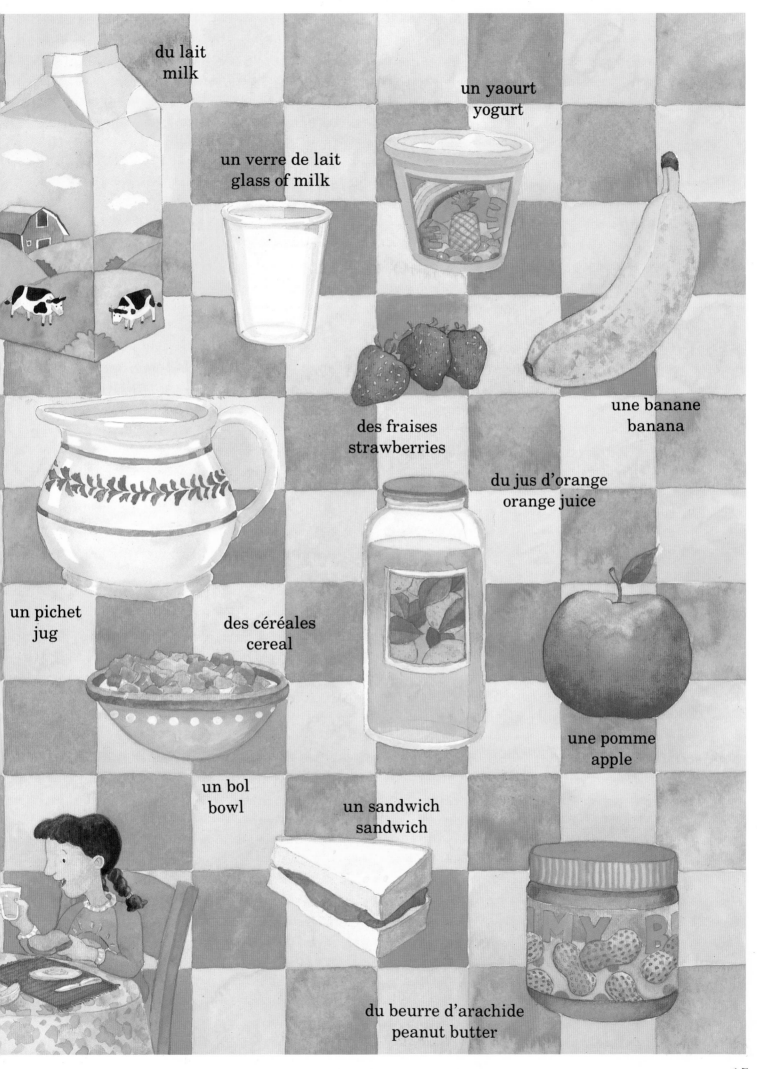

du lait
milk

un yaourt
yogurt

un verre de lait
glass of milk

une banane
banana

des fraises
strawberries

du jus d'orange
orange juice

un pichet
jug

des céréales
cereal

une pomme
apple

un bol
bowl

un sandwich
sandwich

du beurre d'arachide
peanut butter

À l'école
At school

1 2 3 4 5 6 7

un · deux · trois · quatre · cinq · six · sep

Hello        Buon giorno        שלום
Bonjour      Guten Tag          γειά σο
Hola                            喂
                               こんにち

un tableau noir              un professeur
blackboard                   teacher

un globe terrestre           un garçon        une fille
globe                        boy              girl

un microscope
microscope

des livres
books

un aquarium
aquarium

un poisson rouge
goldfish

une batte de base-ball       un pupitre       des élèves
baseball bat                 school desk      students

une cage
cage
                                              un livre
                                              book

un hamster
hamster

un gant de base-ball
baseball mitt

8     9     10

uit     neuf     dix

Bom dia
Goeden Dag
Goddag
Szerbusz

les planètes
planets

une horloge
clock

un calendrier
calendar

un lapin
rabbit

une marionnette
puppet

une carte du monde
map of the world

un piano
piano

un bureau
desk

une guitare
guitar

le soleil
sun

une poubelle
garbage can

une trompette
trumpet

un sac d'écolier
school knapsack

une flûte à bec
flute

un tambour
drum

des patins à roulettes
roller skates

un jeu
game

un tambourin
tambourine

17

# Dans la classe
# In the classroom

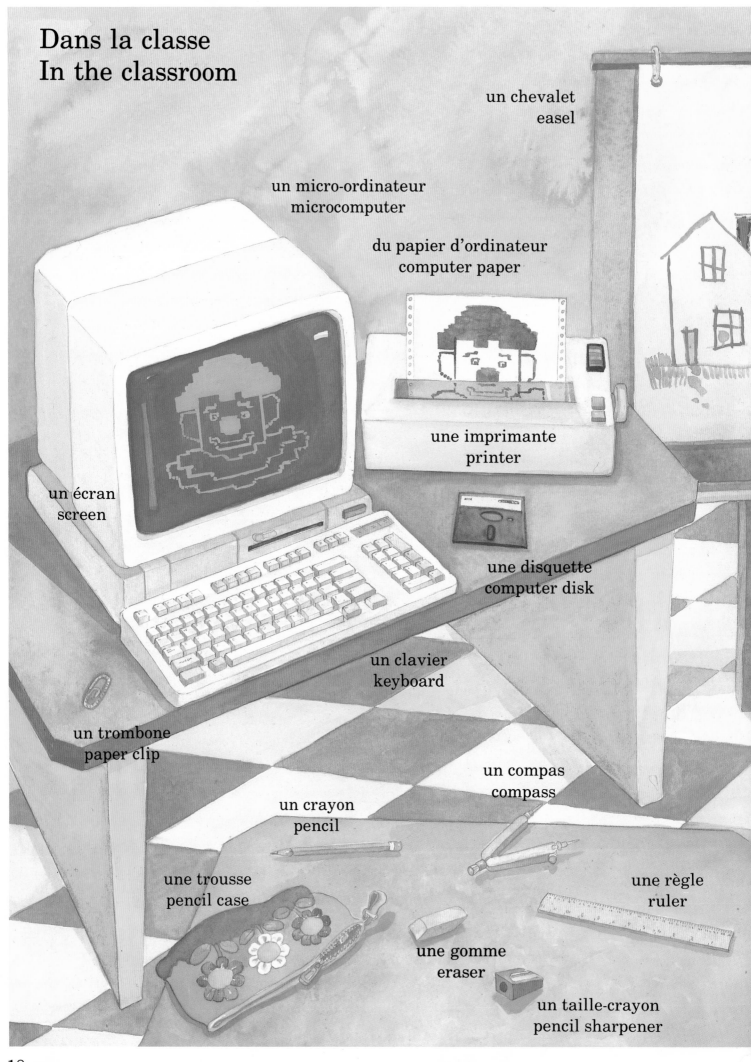

un chevalet
easel

un micro-ordinateur
microcomputer

du papier d'ordinateur
computer paper

une imprimante
printer

un écran
screen

une disquette
computer disk

un clavier
keyboard

un trombone
paper clip

un compas
compass

un crayon
pencil

une trousse
pencil case

une règle
ruler

une gomme
eraser

un taille-crayon
pencil sharpener

un dessin
picture

des crayons de couleur
colored pencils

de la colle
glue

un pot de peinture
can of paint

des crayons gras
crayons

une boîte de couleurs
paint box

un pinceau
paintbrush

du ruban adhésif
tape

des ciseaux
scissors

un dictionnaire
dictionary

une calculatrice
calculator

un stylo
pen

un livre de classe
textbook

un cahier
notebook

1 + 1 = 2
1 + 2 = 3

# Ce que je fais à l'école
# What I do at school

$$1+1 = 2$$
$$1+2 = 3$$
$$1+3 = 4$$

additionner
add

$$4-1 = 3$$
$$3-1 = 2$$
$$2-1 = 1$$

soustraire
subtract

donner à manger aux poissons
feed the fish

compter
count

étudier
study

jouer
play

se balancer
swing

grimper
climb

courir
run

sauter à la corde
skip rope

écrire
write

peindre
paint

dessiner
draw

faire la sieste
nap

21

En excursion
Going on a trip

un gratte-ciel
skyscraper

des nuages
clouds

une ville
city

un village
village

une route
road

un champ
field

une rivièr
river

un car d'école
schoolbus

un zoo
zoo

un épouvantail
scarecrow

une écurie
stable

un éléphant
elephant

une girafe
giraffe

un cygne
swan

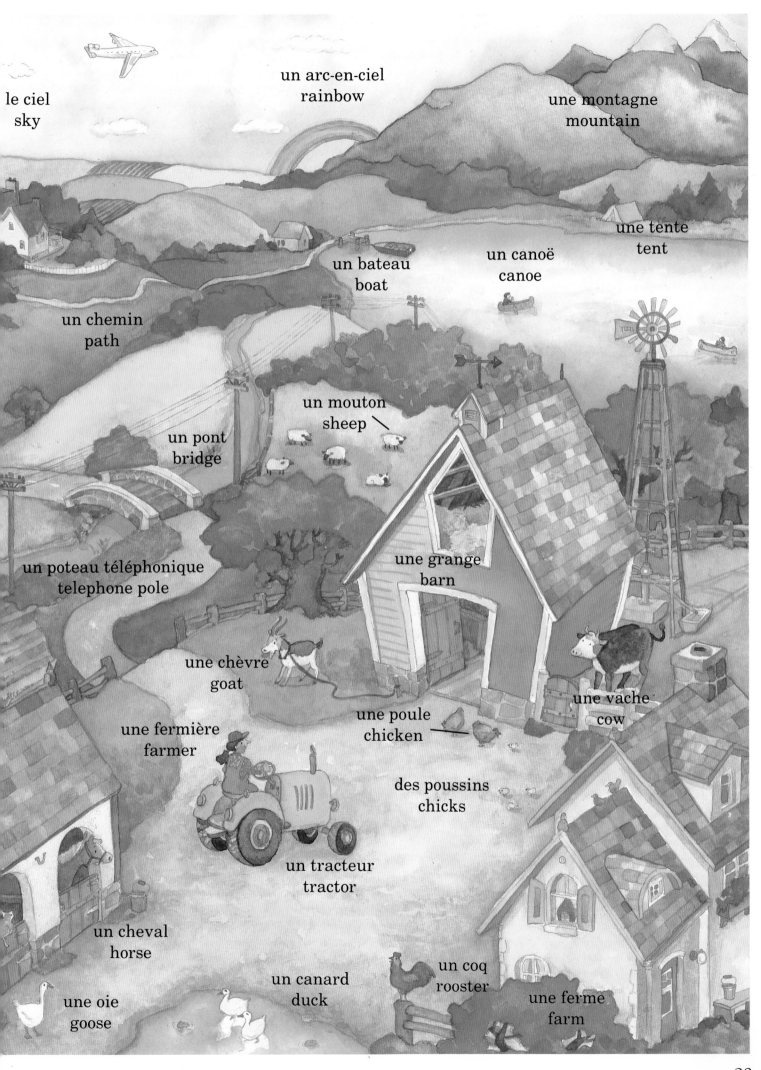

le ciel
sky

un arc-en-ciel
rainbow

une montagne
mountain

une tente
tent

un canoë
canoe

un bateau
boat

un chemin
path

un mouton
sheep

un pont
bridge

une grange
barn

un poteau téléphonique
telephone pole

une chèvre
goat

une vache
cow

une poule
chicken

une fermière
farmer

des poussins
chicks

un tracteur
tractor

un cheval
horse

un coq
rooster

un canard
duck

une oie
goose

une ferme
farm

23

# Au zoo
# At the zoo

un évent
blowhole

une nageoire
flipper

un dauphin
dolphin

une carapace
shell

une tortue
tortoise

un groin
snout

un sanglier
boar

un bec
beak

une aile
wing

un oiseau
bird

la peau
hide

une plume
feather

une trompe d'éléphant
elephant's trunk

une défense d'éléphant
elephant's tusk

des bois
antlers

une queue
tail

un cerf
deer

un mouflon
mountain sheep

une corne
horn

un sabot
hoof

des moustaches
whiskers

un croc
fang

une crinière
mane

une lionne
lioness

le pelage
fur

un ours polaire
polar bear

une patte
paw

une griffe
claw

# Mes animaux préférés au zoo
# My favorite zoo animals

un chameau
camel

un flamant rose
pink flamingo

un phoque
seal

un hippopotame
hippopotamus

un bison
bison

un kangourou
kangaroo

un pingouin
penguin

un gorille
gorilla

un serpent
snake

un singe
monkey

un toucan
toucan

un ours brun
brown bear

un crocodile
crocodile

une souris
mouse

un perroquet
parrot

un lion
lion

un tigre
tiger

une baleine
whale

À la ville
In the city

un appartement
apartment

une banque
bank

un coiffeur
hairdresser

une librairie
bookstore

une peinture murale
mural

un hôtel
hotel

une poissonnerie
fish store

une boucherie
butcher shop

une épicerie
grocery store

un trottoir
sidewalk

un taxi
taxi

une cabine téléphonique
phone booth

un agent de police
police officer

un bureau de poste
post office

un banc
park bench

un accident
accident

une fontaine
fountain

un jardin public
park

une boîte aux lettres
mailbox

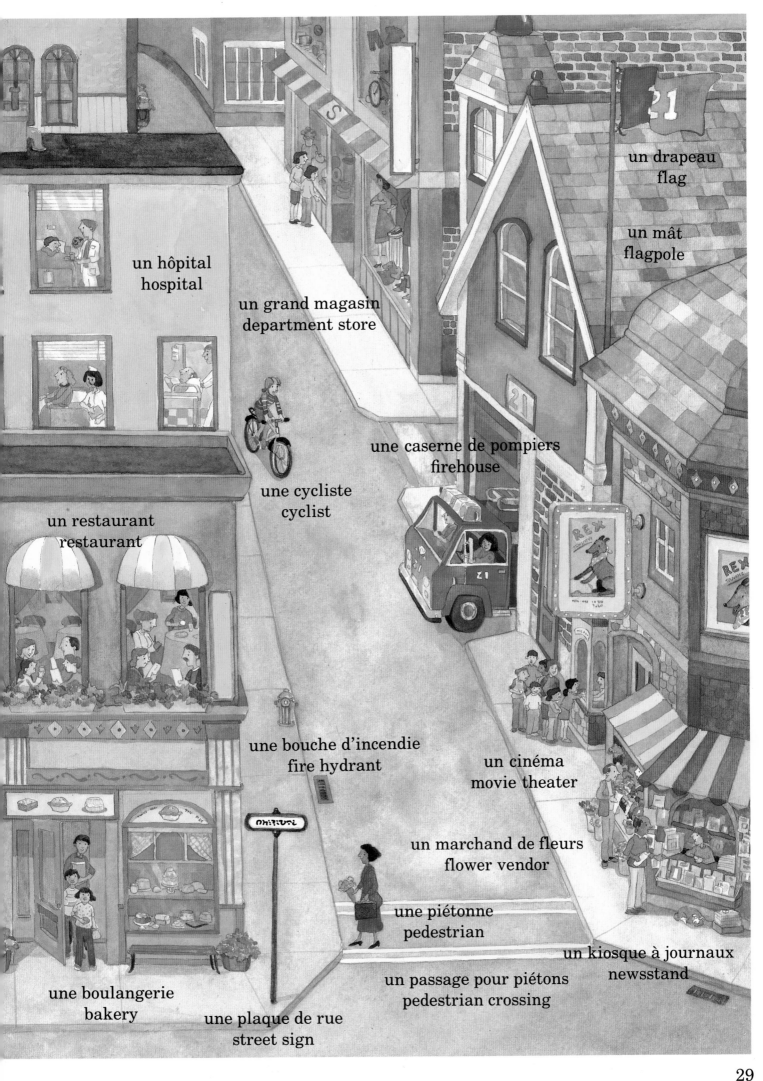

un hôpital
hospital

un grand magasin
department store

un drapeau
flag

un mât
flagpole

une caserne de pompiers
firehouse

une cycliste
cyclist

un restaurant
restaurant

une bouche d'incendie
fire hydrant

un cinéma
movie theater

un marchand de fleurs
flower vendor

une piétonne
pedestrian

un kiosque à journaux
newsstand

un passage pour piétons
pedestrian crossing

une boulangerie
bakery

une plaque de rue
street sign

# Au magasin
# At the store

une caissière
cashier

du céleri
celery

une cliente
customer

une caisse
cash register

un sac en papier
paper bag

une banane
banana

un citron
lemon

un ananas
pineapple

une pêche
peach

une pomme
apple

une orange
orange

un pamplemousse
grapefruit

une poire
pear

un abricot
apricot

une framboise
raspberry

une prune
plum

une mangue
mango

une cerise
cherry

une pastèque
watermelon

des raisins
grapes

un avocat
avocado

des pois
peas

une laitue
lettuce

un concombre
cucumber

un épicier
grocer

une tomate
tomato

une carotte
carrot

un oignon
onion

une pomme de terre
potato

du maïs
corn

des haricots verts
green beans

# Les moyens de transport
# Means of transportation

une ambulance
ambulance

un hélicoptère
helicopter

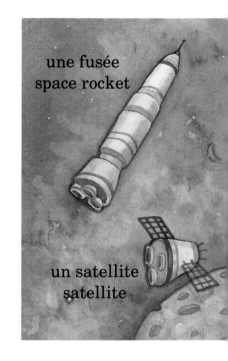

une fusée
space rocket

un satellite
satellite

un paquebot
steamship

un voilier
sailboat

un bateau à moteur
motor boat

une planche à voile
windsurfer

un tricycle
tricycle

une voiture de sport
sportscar

une dépanneuse
tow truck

un camion
truck

un jet
jet

un avion
plane

un autobus
bus

un train
train

une bicyclette
bicycle

un chariot
wagon

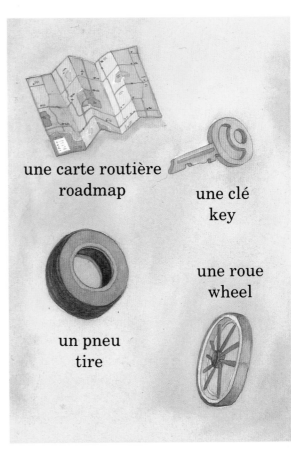

une carte routière
roadmap

une clé
key

une roue
wheel

un pneu
tire

un camion de livraison
delivery truck

une remorque
trailer

un camping-car
motor home

# Dans mon jardin
# In my backyard

un seau
pail

une pelle
shovel

un râteau
rake

un parasol de jardin
garden umbrella

un bac à sable
sandbox

un pissenlit
dandelion

une chaise de jardin
garden chair

une planche à roulettes
skateboard

un géranium
geranium

un papillon
butterfly

une libellule
dragonfly

une fourmi
ant

une mouche
fly

une terrasse
deck

un barbecue
barbecue

du charbon de bois
charcoal

34

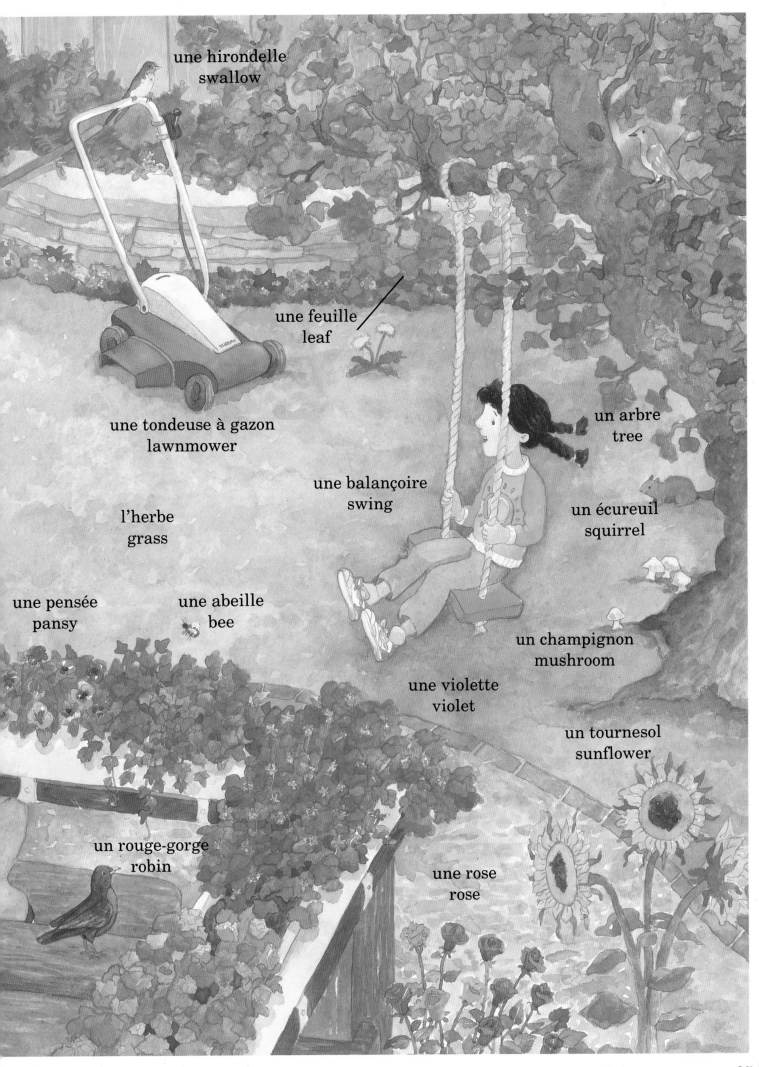

une hirondelle
swallow

une feuille
leaf

une tondeuse à gazon
lawnmower

un arbre
tree

une balançoire
swing

l'herbe
grass

un écureuil
squirrel

une pensée
pansy

une abeille
bee

un champignon
mushroom

une violette
violet

un tournesol
sunflower

un rouge-gorge
robin

une rose
rose

# On mange des grillades
# Barbecue time

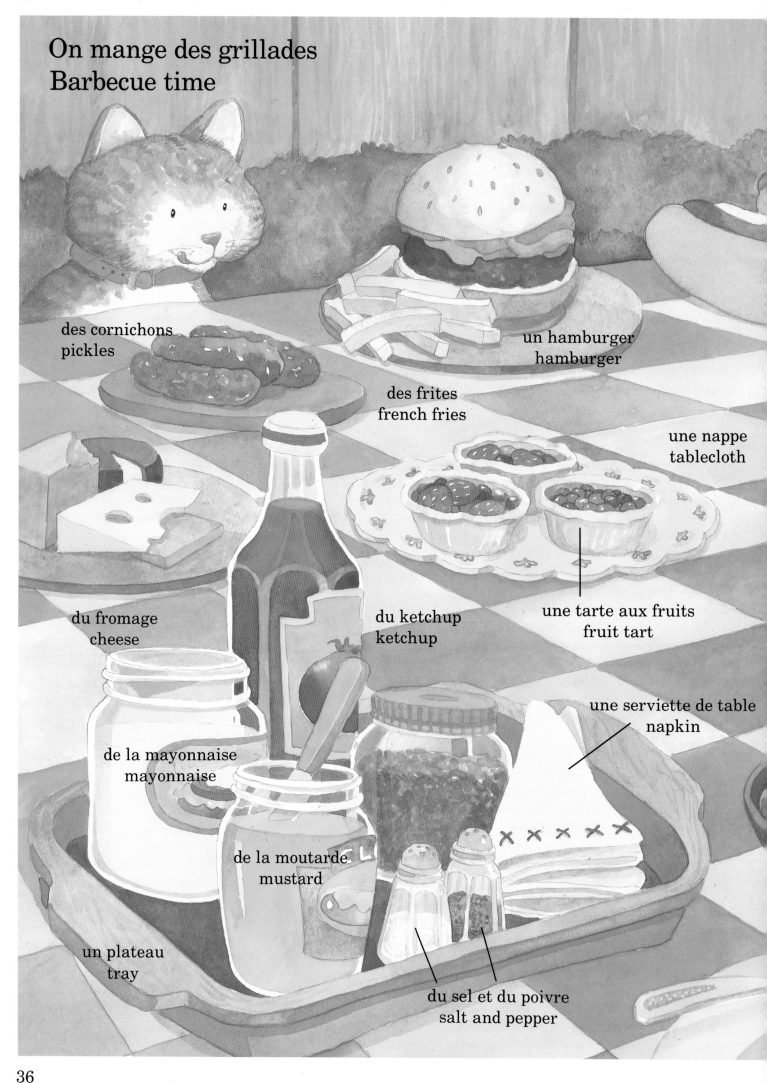

des cornichons
pickles

un hamburger
hamburger

des frites
french fries

une nappe
tablecloth

du fromage
cheese

du ketchup
ketchup

une tarte aux fruits
fruit tart

de la mayonnaise
mayonnaise

une serviette de table
napkin

de la moutarde
mustard

un plateau
tray

du sel et du poivre
salt and pepper

des hot-dogs
hot dogs

une table
table

de la glace
ice cream

des biscuits
cookies

du gâteau
cake

une salade de fruits
fruit salad

une corbeille de fruits
basket of fruit

un jus de fruit
fruit juice

une boisson gazeuse
soda pop

une salade
salad

# Mes couleurs préférées
# My favorite colors

rose
pink

orange
orange

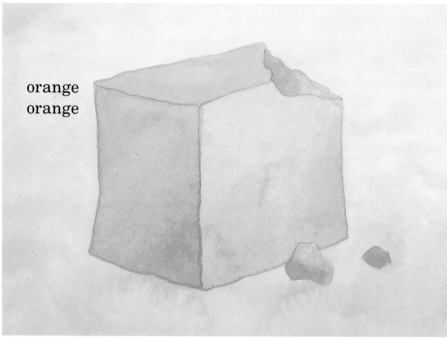

rouge
red

marron
brown

noir
black

vert
green

beige
beige

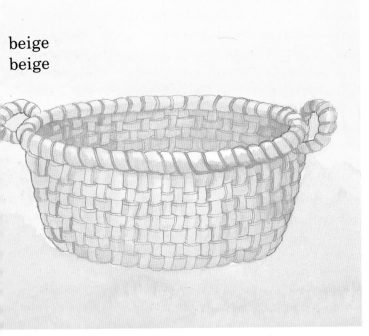

jaune
yellow

bleu
blue

gris
gray

violet
purple

blanc
white

39

De ma fenêtre
From my window

une étoile
star

une maison
house

une piscine
pool

un raton laveur
raccoon

une échelle
ladder

une poussette
stroller

une cabane dans un arbre
treehouse

un trottoir
sidewalk

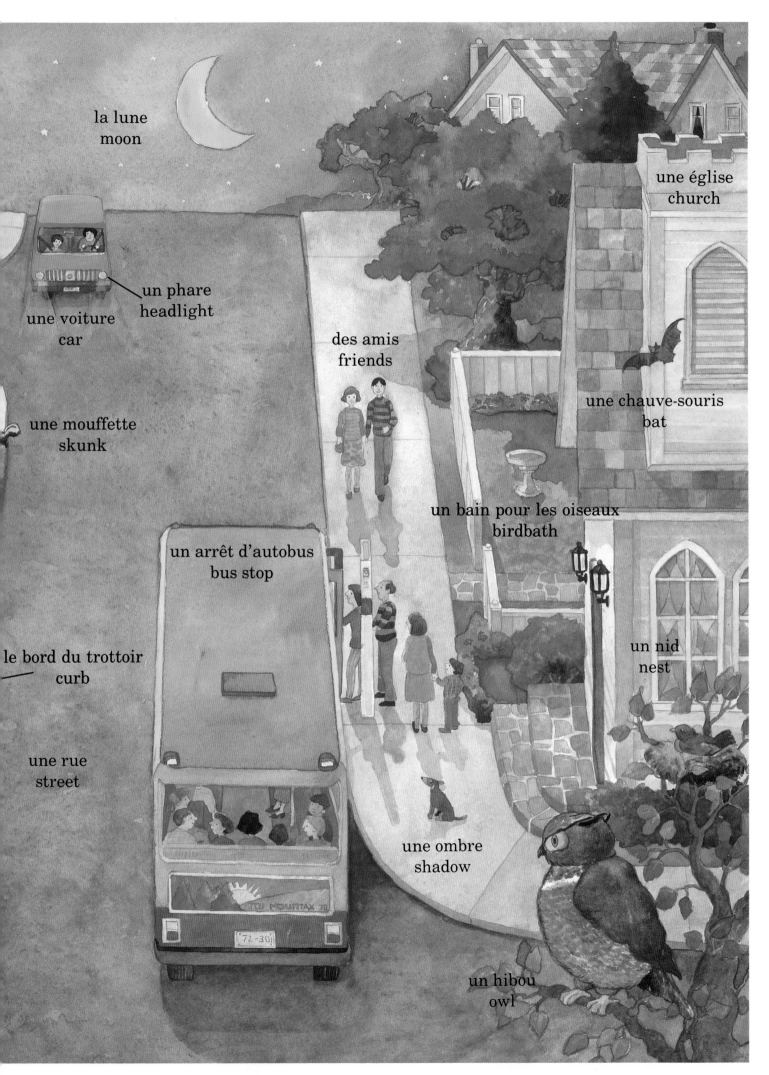

la lune
moon

un phare
headlight

une voiture
car

une mouffette
skunk

le bord du trottoir
curb

un arrêt d'autobus
bus stop

une rue
street

des amis
friends

une église
church

une chauve-souris
bat

un bain pour les oiseaux
birdbath

un nid
nest

une ombre
shadow

un hibou
owl

Bonne nuit!
Good night!

un store
blind

un dessin
drawing

une photo
photo

un vase de fleurs
flower vase

une lampe
lamp

un lit
bed

un drap
sheet

un réveille-matin
alarm clock

une couverture
blanket

un tiroir
drawer

une commode
chest of drawers

des oreillers
pillows

un tapis
carpet

une brosse à cheveux
hair brush

une chaise
chair

un fauteuil à bascule
rocking chair

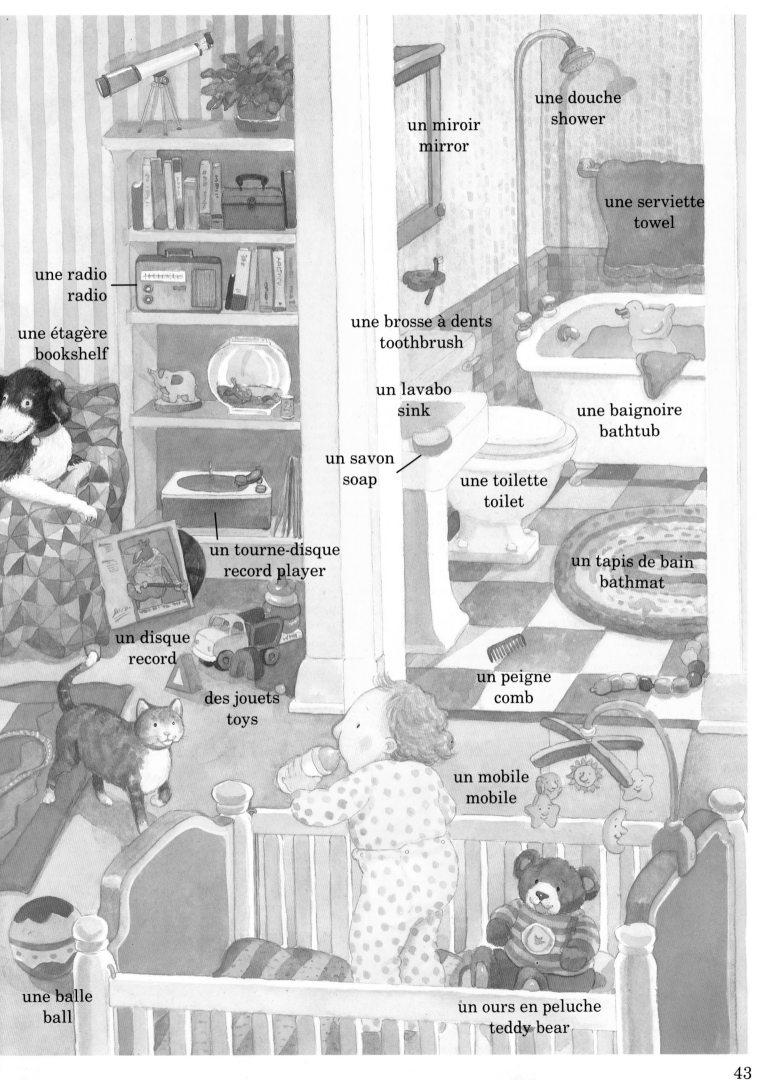

une radio
radio

une étagère
bookshelf

un tourne-disque
record player

un disque
record

des jouets
toys

une balle
ball

un miroir
mirror

une douche
shower

une serviette
towel

une brosse à dents
toothbrush

un lavabo
sink

une baignoire
bathtub

un savon
soap

une toilette
toilet

un tapis de bain
bathmat

un peigne
comb

un mobile
mobile

un ours en peluche
teddy bear

43

# Quel est le contraire?
# What's the opposite?

haut
high

bas
low

carré
square

rond
round

sur
on

sous
under

froid
cold

chaud
hot

plein
full

vide
empty

mou
soft

sec
dry

mouillé
wet

dur
hard

propre
clean

sale
dirty

ouvert
open

fermé
closed

grand
big

petit
small

heureux
happy

triste
sad

45

# Pronunciation Guide

Note: (n) means that the vowel before it is nasalized. The (n) itself is not said.

▶A

abeille  *ah-BAY-yuh*
abricot  *ah-bree-CO*
accident  *ahx-ee-DAHN*
additionner  *ah-deece-yo-NAY*
agent de police  *ah-ZHAH(n) duh po-LEECE*
aile  *el*
À la ville  *ah lah VEEL*
À l'école  *ah lay-COLL*
ambulance  *ah(n)-bew-LAH(n)CE*
amis  *ah-MEE*
ananas  *ah-nah-NAH*
appartement  *ah-par-tuh-MAH(n)*
aquarium  *ah-kwar-YUM*
arbre  *AR-br*
arc-en-ciel  *ar-kah(n)s-YELL*
arrêt d'autobus  *ah-RAY doh-toe-BEWS*
arrière-grand-mère  *ahr-YAIR grah(n)-MAIR*
arrière-grand-père  *ahr-YAIR grah(n)-PAIR*
arroser les plantes  *ah-ro-ZAY lay PLAH(n)T*
assiette  *ah-see-ET*
Au magasin  *oh mah-gah-ZA(n)*
autobus  *oh-toe-BEWS*
Au zoo  *oh ZO*
avion  *ahv-YO(n)*
avocat  *ah-vo-KAH*

▶B

bac à sable  *bahk ah SAH-bl*
baignoire  *bay-NWAHR*
bain pour les oiseaux  *ba(n) poor lay zwah-ZO*
balançoire  *bah-lah(n)-SWAHR*
baleine  *bah-LEN*
balle  *bahl*
banane  *bah-NAHN*
banc  *bah(n)*
banque  *bah(n)k*
barbecue  *bar-be-CUE*
bardeaux  *bar-DOE*
bas  *bah*
bateau  *bah-TOE*
bateau à moteur  *bah-toe ah mo-TER*
batte de base-ball  *baht duh bez-BAHL*
bébé  *bay-BAY*
bec  *beck*
beige  *bezh*
beurre  *ber*
beurre d'arachide  *ber dah-rah-SHEED*
bicyclette  *bee-see-CLET*
Bienvenue chez moi  *bee-a(n)-vuh-NEW shay mwah*
biscuits  *beece-KWEE*
bison  *bee-ZO(n)*
blanc  *blah(n)*
bleu  *bluh*
blouson  *bloo-ZO(n)*
boire  *bwar*
bois  *bwah*
boisson gazeuse  *bwah-SO(n) gah-ZUHZ*
boîte aux lettres  *bwaht oh LET-tr*
boîte de couleurs  *bwaht duh coo-LER*
bol  *bol*
Bonjour  *bo(n)-ZHOOR*
Bonne nuit  *bun NWEE*

bonnet  *bo-NAY*
bord du trottoir  *bor dew tro-TWAR*
bottes  *boht*
bouche  *boosh*
bouche d'incendie  *boosh da(n)-sah(n)-DEE*
boucherie  *boo-SHREE*
boulangerie  *boo-lah(n)-ZHREE*
bras  *brah*
brosse à cheveux  *bross ah shuh-VUH*
brosse à dents  *bross ah dah(n)*
brunette  *brew-NET*
bureau  *bewr-O*
bureau de poste  *bewr-o duh POST*

▶C

cabane dans un arbre  *cah-bahn dah(n)z uhn AR-br*
cabine téléphonique  *cah-BEAN tay-lay-phone-EEK*
cage  *cah-zh*
cahier  *cah-YAY*
caisse  *kess*
caissière  *kess-YAIR*
calculatrice  *cahl-kew-lah-TREECE*
calendrier  *cah-lah(n)-dree-AY*
camion  *cah-mee-O(n)*
camion de livraison  *cah-mee-o(n) duh lee-vray-ZO(n)*
camping-car  *cah(n)-ping-CAR*
canard  *cah-NAR*
canoë  *cah-no-AY*
carapace  *cah-rah-PAHS*
car d'école  *car day-COLL*
carotte  *ca-ROT*
carré  *ca-RAY*
carte du monde  *cart dew mo(n)d*
carte routière  *cart root-YAIR*
caserne de pompiers  *cah-zayrn duh po(n)-PYAY*
ceinture  *sa(n)-TEWR*
céleri  *sell-REE*
Ce que je fais à l'école  *suh kuh zhuh fay ah lay-COLL*
céréales  *say-ray-AL*
cerf  *sair*
cerise  *suh-REEZ*
C'est le matin  *say luh ma-TA(n)*
chaise  *shayz*
chaise de jardin  *shayz duh zhar-DA(n)*
chambre  *SHAH(n)-br*
chameau  *shah-MOE*
champ  *shah(n)*
champignon  *shah(n)-peen-YO(n)*
chapeau  *shah-POE*
charbon de bois  *shar-bo(n) duh BWA*
chariot  *shahr-YO*
chat  *shah*
chaud  *sho*
chaussettes  *sho-SET*
chaussures de sport  *sho-sewr duh SPOR*
chauve-souris  *shoav-soo-REE*
chemin  *shuh-MA(n)*
cheminée  *shuh-mee-NAY*
chemise  *shuh-MEEZ*
chemise de nuit  *shuh-meez duh NWEE*
cheval  *shuh-VAHL*
chevalet  *shuh-vah-LAY*
cheveux  *shuh-VUH*

cheveux blonds  *shuh-vuh BLO(n)*
cheveux châtains  *shuh-vuh sha-TA(n)*
cheveux roux  *shuh-vuh ROO*
cheville  *shuh-VEE-yuh*
chèvre  *SHEV-r*
chien  *shee-A(n)*
ciel  *see-EL*
cil  *seel*
cinéma  *see-nay-MAH*
cinq  *sa(n)k*
ciseaux  *see-ZO*
citron  *see-TRO(n)*
clavier  *clahv-YAY*
clé  *clay*
cliente  *cli-AH(n)T*
clôture  *clo-TEWR*
coiffeur  *cwah-FER*
colle  *coll*
commode  *co-MOHD*
compas  *co(n)-PAH*
compter  *co(n)-TAY*
concombre  *co(n)-CO(n)-br*
coq  *cock*
corbeille de fruits  *cor-bay-yuh duh FRWEE*
corde à linge  *cord ah LA(n)ZH*
corne  *corn*
cornichons  *cor-nee-SHO(n)*
cou  *coo*
coude  *cood*
courir  *coo-REER*
cousin  *coo-ZA(n)*
cousine  *coo-ZEEN*
couteau  *coo-TOE*
couverture  *coo-vair-TEWR*
crayon  *cray-O(n)*
crayons de couleur  *cray-o(n) duh coo-LER*
crayons gras  *cray-o(n) GRAH*
crinière  *cree-nee-YAIR*
croc  *cro*
crocodile  *cro-co-DEEL*
croissants  *krwah-SAH(n)*
cuillère  *kwee-YAIR*
cuisine  *kwee-ZEEN*
culotte  *kew-LOT*
cycliste  *see-CLEEST*
cygne  *SEEN-yuh*

▶D

Dans la classe  *dah(n) la CLAHS*
Dans mon jardin  *dah(n) mo(n) zhar-DA(n)*
dauphin  *doe-FA(n)*
défense d'éléphant  *day-FAH(n)S day-lay-FAH(n)*
de la  *duh lah*
De ma fenêtre  *duh mah fuh-NET-r*
dent  *dah(n)*
dépanneuse  *day-pa(h)-NUHZ*
des  *day*
descendre l'escalier  *day-SAH(n)-dr less-cahl-YAY*
dessin  *day-SA(n)*
dessiner  *day-see-NAY*
deux  *duh*
dictionnaire  *deex-yo-NAIR*
disque  *deesk*
disquette  *dees-KET*

46

dix *deece*
doigt *dwah*
donner à manger aux poissons *doe-nay ah mah(n)-ZHAY oh pwah-SO(n)*
dormir *dor-MEER*
dos *doe*
douche *doosh*
drap *drah*
drapeau *drah-PO*
du *dew*
dur *dewr*

▶E
écharpe *ay-SHARP*
échelle *ay-SHELL*
écran *ay-CRAH(n)*
écrire *ay-CREER*
écureuil *ay-kew-ROY-uh*
écurie *ay-kew-REE*
église *ay-GLEEZ*
éléphant *ay-lay-FAH(n)*
élèves *ay-LEV*
En excursion *ah(n) nex-kewrs-YO(n)*
épaule *ay-POLE*
épicerie *ay-piece-REE*
épicier *ay-piece-YAY*
épouvantail *ay-poo-vah(n)-TIE*
escalier *ess-cahl-YAY*
étagère *ay-tah-ZHAIR*
étoile *ay-TWAHL*
étudier *ay-tewd-YAY*
évent *ay-VAH(n)*

▶F
faire frire un oeuf *fair freer uh(n) NUHF*
faire la sieste *fair lah see-EST*
fauteuil à bascule *fo-toy ah bah-SKEWL*
fenêtre *fuh-NET-r*
ferme *fairm*
fermé *fair-MAY*
fermière *fairm-YAIR*
feuille *FOY-uh*
fille *FEE-yuh*
flamant rose *flah-MAH(n) rose*
flûte à bec *flew tah beck*
fontaine *fo(n)-TEN*
fourchette *foor-SHET*
fourmi *foor-MEE*
fraises *frezz*
framboise *frah(n)-BWAHZ*
frère *frair*
frites *freet*
froid *frwah*
fromage *fro-MAH-zh*
fusée *few-ZAY*

▶G
gant de base-ball *gah(n) duh bez-BAHL*
garage *gah-RAH-zh*
garçon *gar-SO(n)*
gâteau *ga-TOE*
genou *zhuh-NOO*
géranium *zhay-rahn-YUM*
gilet *zhee-LAY*
girafe *zhee-RAHF*
glace *glahss*
globe oculaire *globe o-kew-LAIR*
globe terrestre *globe tay-RESS-tr*
gomme *gum*
gorille *gor-EE-yuh*
grand *grah(n)*
grand magasin *grah(n) mah-gah-ZA(n)*
grand-mère *grah(n)-MAIR*
grand-père *grah(n)-PAIR*

grange *grah(n)zh*
gratte-ciel *graht-see-EL*
griffe *greef*
grille-pain *gree-yuh-PA(n)*
grimper *gra(n)-PAY*
gris *gree*
groin *grwa(n)*
guitare *ghee-TAR*

▶H
hamburger *ah(n)-bur-GAIR*
hamster *ahm-STAIR*
haricots verts *ah-ree-co VAIR*
haut *oh*
hélicoptère *ay-lee-cop-TAIR*
herbe *airb*
heureux *uh-RUH*
hibou *ee-BOO*
hippopotame *ee-po-po-TAHM*
hirondelle *ee-ro(n)-DELL*
hôpital *o-pee-TAHL*
horloge *or-LOZH*
hot-dogs *ot-DOG*
hôtel *o-TELL*
huit *weet*

▶I
imprimante *a(n)-pree-MAH(n)T*

▶J
jambe *zhah(n)-b*
jardin public *zhar-DA(n) pew-BLEEK*
jardinière *zhar-deen-YAIR*
jaune *zhone*
jet *zhay*
jeu *zhuh*
joue *zhoo*
jouer *zhoo-AY*
jouets *zhoo-AY*
jumelles *zhew-MEL*
jupe *zhewp*
jus de fruit *zhew duh FRWEE*
jus d'orange *zhew dor-AH(n)ZH*

▶K
kangourou *kah(n)-goo-ROO*
ketchup *ket-SHUHP*
kiosque à journaux *kee-ohs kah zhoor-NO*

▶L
la *lah*
lacets *lah-SAY*
lait *lay*
laitue *lay-TEW*
lampe *lah(n)p*
langue *lah(n)g*
lapin *la-PA(n)*
lavabo *lah-vah-BO*
le *luh*
les *lay*
Les moyens de transport *lay-mwah-ya(n) duh trah(n)-SPORT*
libellule *lee-bay-LEWL*
librairie *lee-bray-REE*
lion *lee-O(n)*
lionne *lee-UN*
lire *leer*
lit *lee*
livre(s) *LEE-vr*
livre de classe *lee-vr duh CLAHS*
lune *lewn*

▶M
maillot de corps *mah-yo duh COR*
main *ma(n)*
maïs *mah-EECE*
maison *may-ZO(n)*

manger *mah(n)-ZHAY*
mangue *mah(n)g*
manteau *mah(n)-TOE*
marchand de fleurs *mar-shah(n) duh FLER*
marcher *mar-SHAY*
marionnette *mahr-yo-NET*
marron *mah-RO(n)*
mayonnaise *mah-yo-NAIZ*
mât *mah*
menton *mah(n)-TO(n)*
mère *mair*
Mes animaux préférés au zoo *may zah-nee-MOE pray-fay-RAY oh ZO*
Mes couleurs préférés *may coo-LER pray-fay-RAY*
micro-ordinateur *mee-cro-or-dee-nah-TER*
microscope *mee-cro-SCOP*
miroir *meer-WAHR*
mitaine *mee-TEN*
mobile *mo-BEEL*
Mon corps *mo(n) COR*
montagne *mo(n)-TAHN-yuh*
monter l'escalier *mo(n)-tay less-cahl-YAY*
mou *moo*
mouche *moosh*
mouffette *moo-FET*
moufle *MOO-fl*
mouflon *moo-FLO(n)*
mouillé *moo-YAY*
moustaches *moo-STAHSH*
moutarde *moo-TARD*
mouton *moo-TO(n)*
mur *mewr*

▶N
nageoire *nah-ZHWAHR*
nappe *nahp*
neuf *nuhf*
neveu *nuh-VUH*
nez *nay*
nid *nee*
nièce *nee-ESS*
noir *nwahr*
nombril *no(n)-BREEL*
nuages *new-AH-zh*

▶O
oeil *OY-yuh*
oeuf *uhf*
oie *wah*
oignon *on-YO(n)*
oiseau *wah-ZO*
ombre *O(n)-br*
oncle *O(n)-cl*
On déjeune *o(n) day-ZHUN*
ongle *O(n)-gl*
On mange des grillades *o(n) mah(n)zh day gree-YAHD*
orange *or-AH(n)ZH*
oreille *or-AY-yuh*
oreillers *or-ay-YAY*
orteil *or-TAY-yuh*
ours brun *oorce BRUH(n)*
ours en peluche *oorce ah(n) puh-LEWSH*
ours polaire *oorce po-LAIR*
ouvert *oo-VAIR*

▶P
pain grillé *pa(n) gree-YAY*
pamplemousse *pah(n)-pluh-MOOSE*
pantalon *pah(n)-tah-LO(n)*
pantoufles *pah(n)-TOO-fl*

papier d'ordinateur *pahp-yay dor-dee-nah-TER*
papillon *pah-pee-YO(n)*
paquebot *pahk-BOE*
parasol de jardin *pah-rah-SOL duh zhar-DA(n)*
parents *pah-RAH(n)*
passage pour piétons *pah-SAH-zh poor pyay-TO(n)*
pastèque *pah-STEK*
patins à roulettes *pa-ta(n) ah roo-LET*
patte *pat*
paupière *pope-YAIR*
peau *poe*
pêche *pesh*
peigne *PAIN-yuh*
peignoir *pay-NWAHR*
peindre *PA(n)-dr*
peinture murale *pa(n)-tewr mew-RAHL*
pelage *puh-LAH-zh*
pelle *pell*
pensée *pah(n)-SAY*
père *pair*
perron *pay-RO(n)*
perroquet *pay-ro-KAY*
petit *puh-TEE*
phare *far*
phoque *fock*
photo *fo-TOE*
piano *pee-ah-NO*
pichet *pee-SHAY*
pied *pyay*
piétonne *pyay-TUN*
pinceau *pa(n)-SO*
pingouin *pa(n)-GWA(n)*
piscine *pee-SEEN*
pissenlit *pee-sah(n)-LEE*
planche à roulettes *plah(n)sh ah roo-LET*
planche à voile *plah(n)sh ah VWAHL*
planètes *plah-NET*
plaque de rue *plahk duh REW*
plateau *plah-TOE*
plein *pla(n)*
pleurer *pluh-RAY*
plume *plewm*
pneu *p-NUH*
poignet *pwahn-YAY*
poire *pwahr*
pois *pwah*
poissonnerie *pwah-sohn-REE*
poisson rouge *pwah-so(n) ROOZH*
pomme *pumm*
pomme de terre *pumm duh TAIR*
pont *po(n)*
porche *porsh*
porte *port*
portillon *por-tee-YO(n)*
pot de peinture *po duh pa(n)-TEWR*
poteau téléphonique *po-TOE tay-lay-phone-EEK*
poubelle *poo-BEL*
pouce *pooce*
poule *pool*
poussette *poo-SET*
poussins *poo-SA(n)*
prendre un bain *prah(n)-druh(n) BA(n)*
prendre une douche *prah(n)-drewn DOOSH*
professeur *pro-fay-SEWR*
propre *PRO-pr*

prune *prewn*
pull-over *pewl-o-VAIR*
pupille *pew-PEE-yuh*
pupitre *pew-PEE-tr*
pyjama *pee-zhah-MAH*

▶Q
quatre *KA-tr*
Quel est le contraire *kel ay luh co(n)-TRAIR*
queue *kuh*

▶R
radio *rahd-YO*
raisins *ray-ZA(n)*
râteau *rah-TOE*
raton laveur *rah-to(n) lah-VER*
regarder la télé *ruh-gar-day lah tay-LAY*
règle *RAY-gl*
remorque *ruh-MORK*
repasser *ruh-pah-SAY*
restaurant *res-toe-RAH(n)*
réveille-matin *ray-vay-yuh ma-TA(n)*
rire *rear*
rivière *reeve-YAIR*
robe *rohb*
rond *ro(n)*
rose *rose*
roue *roo*
rouge *roozh*
rouge-gorge *roozh-gorzh*
roulotte *roo-LOT*
route *root*
ruban adhésif *rew-bah(n) ah-day-ZEEF*
rue *rew*

▶S
s'asseoir *sah-SWAHR*
sabot *sah-BOE*
sac d'écolier *sahk day-coll-YAY*
sac en papier *sah-kah(n) pahp-YAY*
salade *sah-LAHD*
salade de fruits *sah-lahd duh FRWEE*
salle *sahl*
salle à manger *sahl ah mah(n)-ZHAY*
salle de bain *sahl duh ba(n)*
salon *sah-LO(n)*
sandwich *sah(n)d-WEECH*
sanglier *sah(n)-glee-AY*
satellite *sah-tay-LEET*
sauter à la corde *so-tay ah lah CORD*
savon *sah-VO(n)*
seau *so*
se balancer *suh bah-lah(n)-SAY*
se battre *suh BAH-tr*
se brosser les dents *suh bro-say lay DAH(n)*
sec *seck*
se sécher les cheveux *suh say-shay lay shuh-VUH*
sel et poivre *sell ay PWAH-vr*
sept *set*
serpent *sair-PAH(n)*
serviette *sair-vee-ET*
serviette de table *sair-vee-et duh TAH-bl*
short *short*
singe *sa(n)zh*
six *seece*
soeur *sir*
soleil *so-LAY-yuh*
souliers *sool-YAY*
sourcil *soor-SEEL*
souris *soo-REE*

sous *soo*
sous-sol *soo-SOL*
soustraire *soo-STRAIR*
store *stor*
stylo *stee-LO*
sucre *SOO-cr*
sur *sewr*
sweat-shirt *sweet-SHUHRT*

▶T
table *TAH-bl*
tableau noir *tah-blo NWAHR*
taille-crayon *tie-cray-O(n)*
tambour *tah(n)-BOOR*
tambourin *tah(n)-boor-A(n)*
tante *tah(n)t*
tapis *tah-PEE*
tapis de bain *tah-pee duh BA(n)*
tarte aux fruits *tart oh FRWEE*
tasse *tahss*
taxi *tack-SEE*
tee-shirt *tee-SHUHRT*
tente *tah(n)t*
terrasse *tay-RAHSS*
tête *tet*
théière *tay-YAIR*
tigre *TEE-gr*
tiroir *teer-WAHR*
toilette *twah-LET*
toit *twah*
tomate *toe-MAHT*
tomber *to(n)-BAY*
tondeuse à gazon *to(n)-duh zah gah-ZO(n)*
tondre la pelouse *to(n)-dr lah puh-LOOZ*
tortue *tor-TEW*
toucan *too-CAH(n)*
tourne-disque *tour-nuh-DEESK*
tournesol *tour-nuh-SOL*
tracteur *trahk-TER*
train *tra(n)*
tricycle *tree-SEE-cl*
triste *treest*
trois *trwah*
trombone *tro(n)-BONE*
trompe d'éléphant *tro(n)p day-lay-FAH(n)*
trompette *tro(n)-PET*
trottoir *tro-TWAHR*
trousse *troos*

▶U
un *uh(n)*
une *ewn*

▶V
vache *vahsh*
vase de fleurs *vahz duh FLER*
verre de lait *vair duh LAY*
vert *vair*
vide *veed*
village *vee-LAH-zh*
ville *veel*
violet *vee-o-LAY*
violette *vee-o-LET*
Voici ma famille *vwah-see mah fah-MEE-yuh*
voilier *vwahl-YAY*
voiture *vwah-TEWR*
voiture de sport *vwah-tewr duh SPOR*

▶Y
yaourt *yah-OORT*
yeux *yuh*

▶Z
zoo *zo*

48